Garfield's
Guide
To
SUCCESSFUL LIVING

JIM DAVIS

ЯR
RAVETTE PUBLISHING

This edition first published by Ravette Publishing Limited 1999.

Printed and bound for Ravette Publishing Limited,
Unit 3, Tristar Centre
Star Road, Partridge Green
West Sussex RH13 8RA
by STIGE, Italy

ISBN: 1 85304 973 5

"IT'S NINETY DEGREES, GARFIELD, AND PEOPLE ARE DYING OUT THERE"

"BUT NOT ME, GARFIELD. AND DO YOU KNOW WHY?"

"BECAUSE I'M WEARING WET SOCKS!"

"THIS MAN NEEDS A HOBBY"

JIM DAVPS 7-23

"WE LEAD THE DULLEST LIVES"

JIM DAVPS 7-24

"HOW DULL, YOU ASK?"

"HEY, LOOK, GARFIELD! A SEED IN A SEEDLESS GRAPE!"

"DON'T ASK"

© 1990 PAWS, INC.

HERE I SIT, WASTING TIME WATCHING TELEVISION

WHILE OTHERS ARE BUCKLING DOWN, WORKING HARD AND GETTING THINGS DONE

JIM DAVIS 10-16

I'M MORE BORED THAN YOU ARE

ARE NOT!

JIM DAVIS 10-19

YOU'VE HEARD OF THE "FOUNTAIN OF YOUTH"?

SIP

MEET THE NEXT BEST THING!

JIM DAVIS 11-25

WHY WAS I CREATED, GARFIELD?

WHAT IS MY PURPOSE IN LIFE?

SPLOT!

TO GIVE OTHERS HOPE?

JIM DAVIS 11-27

© 1991 PAWS, INC.

AS FAR AS YOU'RE CONCERNED, ALL I'M GOOD FOR IS FEEDING YOU

YOU SAY THAT AS IF IT WERE UNIMPORTANT

7-15

BOY, AM I DEPRESSED

JIM DAVIS 7-16

I KNOW! I'LL INVITE ALL MY FRIENDS TO A PARTY!

GEE, I WAS HOPING FOR A BIGGER TURNOUT

THEN NEXT TIME INVITE YOUR ENEMIES

WELL IF IT ISN'T "MISTER GLUTTONY"

HOW ARE YOU, "MISTER I THINK I'LL EAT TWO DOZEN DOUGHNUTS IN ONE SITTING"?

TAKING A NAP "MISTER STUFF MY FACE TILL I PASS OUT"?

JUST DON'T CALL ME "MISTER LARDO"

JIM DAVIS 2-15

GARFIELD HAS A BAD HABIT OF

HOW ABOUT THIS WEATHER?

INTERRUPTING ME

JIM DAVIS 2-16